An I Can Read Book®

MARIGOLD and GRANDMA ON THE TOWN

story by Stephanie Calmenson
pictures by Mary Chalmers

HarperCollins*Publishers*

To Joanna
—S.C.

To Yum-Yum
—M.C.

I Can Read Book is a registered trademark of HarperCollins Publishers.

MARIGOLD AND GRANDMA ON THE TOWN
Text copyright © 1994 by Stephanie Calmenson
Illustrations copyright © 1994 by Mary Chalmers
Printed in the U.S.A. All rights reserved.

Library of Congress Cataloging-in-Publication Data
Calmenson, Stephanie.
    Marigold and Grandma on the town / story by Stephanie Calmenson ;
pictures by Mary Chalmers.
        p.   cm. — (An I can read book)
    Summary: When they go out on the town together, two bunnies, Marigold
and Grandma, buy a special hat, eat lunch, and make funny faces in
the photo booth.
    ISBN 0-06-020812-0. — ISBN 0-06-020813-9 (lib. bdg.)
    [1. Rabbits—Fiction.]   I. Chalmers, Mary, date, ill.   II. Title.
III. Series.
PZ7.C136Mar   1994   89-31147
[E]—dc19   CIP
                                                                          AC

2   3   4   5   6   7   8   9   10
❖

CONTENTS

THE HAT

Marigold and Grandma

were going to town.

"Would you like a new hat

for spring?" asked Grandma.

"Will it have ribbons and flowers

on it?" asked Marigold.

"If you want ribbons and flowers

you will have them," said Grandma.

Grandma took Marigold

to Duffy's Department Store.

6

They went through

the revolving door,

and up, up, up

to the hats.

There were big hats and small hats,

square hats and round hats.

There were lots of hats

with ribbons and flowers.

"I like the blue one with pink ribbons

and white flowers," said Marigold.

The saleslady took the hat down

and put it on Marigold's head.

"Oh, my, something is not right,"

said Grandma.

"Let's try it this way,"
said the saleslady.
She tucked Marigold's ears
inside the hat.

"That looks better,"

said the saleslady.

"Do you like it?"

Marigold did not say anything.

"Don't you like the hat?"

asked the saleslady again.

Marigold just stood there.

She could not hear a thing.

"I think I know the problem,"

said Grandma.

She took the hat

off Marigold's head.

"Do you like the hat, dear?"

asked Grandma softly.

"Yes I do!" said Marigold.

"We will take it," said Grandma,

"and we would like to borrow

a pair of scissors, please."

Grandma paid for the hat.

Then she cut two holes in it.

"That looks just right,"

said Grandma.

"Oh, yes!" said Marigold.

"It's just what I wanted."

Marigold wore her hat

out of the store.

And she heard every nice word

that was said about it.

15

THE WIND

"Would you like to go to the park
and feed the ducks?" asked Grandma.

"Yes!" said Marigold.

"I will show the ducks
my new hat."

Marigold held her head up high.

Whoosh!

The wind blew Marigold's hat

right off her head.

"My hat! My hat!"
cried Marigold.
Grandma and Marigold
ran after the hat.

19

"I will get it!"

said the pretzel man.

But the hat flew to the right.

"I will get it!"

said a lady selling newspapers.

But the hat flew to the left.

"I think I can get it!"

said a policewoman.

She jumped up and grabbed the hat.

"Thank you!" said Marigold.

"Let's put it in the box for now,"

Grandma said.

"*Quack, quack!*

Quack, quack!"

Marigold heard the ducks.

She ran to the pond.

"Hello, ducks!" said Marigold.

"I have bread for you."

She tossed some bread to the ducks.

Whoosh!

The wind blew the bread

right back to Marigold.

Marigold tried again,

but the same thing happened.

"Go away, wind!

First you blew away my hat.

Now you will not let me

feed the ducks," shouted Marigold.

"Try to make friends with the wind,"

said Grandma.

"I don't think the wind

wants to be my friend,"

said Marigold.

"Maybe it does," said Grandma.

"Maybe the wind will help you

make a wish."

"How?" asked Marigold.

"See those dandelions

across the pond?" asked Grandma.

"You blow on a dandelion

to make a wish.

The farther the seeds fly,

the faster your wish

will come true."

Marigold and Grandma

hurried to the other side

of the pond.

Marigold picked

the fluffiest dandelion

she could find.

Then she closed her eyes

and said softly,

"I wish I could feed the ducks."

Marigold took a big breath

and blew on the dandelion.

Suddenly the wind came up behind Marigold.

Whoosh!

The wind carried the seeds across the pond.

Marigold smiled.

"Grandma!

My wish is going to come true right away," said Marigold.

"Yes, it is," said Grandma.

"The wind just had to be behind you to help."

Marigold tossed the bread again.

Whoosh!

The wind blew the bread

to the ducks.

"*Quack, quack!*" said the ducks

to their new friend, Marigold.

"Thank you," said Marigold

to her new friend, the wind.

WONDERFUL!

"I am hungry," said Marigold.

"Me too," said Grandma.

They walked into Henry's Coffee Shop.

"Yoo-hoo! Henry! Come and meet

my wonderful granddaughter!"

"I will be there in a minute,"

Henry called.

"I have told him all about you,"

said Grandma.

A waiter led Grandma and Marigold
to a table.

"We would like
two egg salad sandwiches,
a cup of tea for me,
and a glass of milk
for my wonderful granddaughter,"
said Grandma.

Marigold sat up extra tall.
She wanted to look wonderful.

"May I have a pickle, Grandma?"

asked Marigold when their lunch came.

"Yes, you may," said Grandma.

Marigold put her paw into the bowl

and swished it around.

"Oh, Marigold!" said Grandma.

"Please use a fork."

"Sorry," said Marigold.

"That was not a wonderful thing

to do," said Marigold to herself.

"I am glad Henry did not see me."

Marigold found a pickle

and ate it in three bites.

Hic! Hic-hic!

She had the hiccups.

Hiccups were not wonderful.

Marigold held her breath

to get rid of them.

Just then, Henry came to the table.

"Hello, Marigold," said Henry.

"I am so glad to meet you."

"Hic!" said Marigold.

43

Henry reached out

to shake Marigold's paw.

When Marigold reached out—

Hic!

Wham!

Milk was everywhere.

Marigold began to cry.

"Don't worry," said Grandma.

"It's all right."

Marigold looked at her lunch.

"I thought you were hungry,"

said Grandma.

"I am not so hungry anymore,"

said Marigold.

"What is the matter?" asked Grandma.

"I was trying to be wonderful,

but I know I was not,"

said Marigold.

"I think you are wonderful

all the time!" said Grandma.

"Really?" asked Marigold.

"Really," said Grandma.

Marigold felt much better.

Henry came back

with a fresh glass of milk

and a big piece of carrot cake.

"I give carrot cake to all

my wonderful customers," said Henry.

Marigold looked at her carrot cake

and started to smile.

"Grandma," said Marigold,

"will I still be wonderful

if I pick up the cake with my paws?

And if I lick the icing off the top?

And if I get icing on my whiskers

and wipe it on my sleeve?"

"You will still be wonderful,"

said Grandma.

"But you will be

in big trouble too."

"Then I will use my fork,"

said Marigold.

She took a bite of the cake.

"How is it?" asked Grandma.

"Wonderful!" said Marigold.

CLICK!

"Home again! Home again!"

sang Grandma and Marigold

as they walked up Willow Street.

53

They liked Willow Street.

They liked to look

in the store windows.

Sometimes they went inside.

There was PETE'S PIZZA.

But they had just had lunch.

There was MY LITTLE CARD SHOP.

But they did not need any cards.

And there was SAY CHEESE,

the photo shop.

"Let's stop here, Marigold,"

said Grandma.

"I want a picture of you

in your new hat."

"Do we have to?" Marigold asked.

Marigold did not want to have

her picture taken.

"It will only take a minute,"

said Grandma.

Marigold made a grumpy face.

She rolled her eyes way up.

She pushed her eyebrows way down.

She turned the corners of her mouth

down to her chin.

Grandma looked at Marigold
and smiled.

"That is a perfect face," she said.

They walked into the photo booth.

Grandma closed the curtains.

"Would you like

to put in the quarters?"

asked Grandma.

Marigold put the quarters

into the machine.

A red light blinked.

"Ready!" said Grandma.

"Grumpy faces!"

Click!

"Silly faces!" said Marigold.

Click!

"Smile!" said Grandma.

Click!

"Hug!" said Marigold.

Click!

And that was the best picture of all.